The Luckiest Boy

Musings of being born and raised in Belgrade Lakes in the 50's and 60's

By Rod Johnson,
The Luckiest Boy

Front cover shows Long Pond from just below the dam in Belgrade Lakes, and a lucky boy. Back cover photo is of the author.

Contents

Dedication

To the ancestors who lived on this land, and to those who
strive to protect it today.

Introduction

Welcome. The Luckiest Boy is a 12 Chapter collection of childhood memories—as recalled by author Rod Johnson. The stories collectively portray youthful adventures while growing up in the small Maine town of Belgrade Lakes.

The era is early 1950's thru mid 1960's. You'll be living through the eyes and mind, and experiencing the adventures of youth who had the good fortune and freedom to be raised by good parents and a village of caring folks.

In addition to these stories we've included some photos, found in various attics around Main street. Also included are some direct favorite quotes from the story's characters and a host of good old sayings, some you've heard and some haven't. To be politically correct we must tell you that swear words appear now and then, but nothing really lewd.

Our hopes are that you enjoy these recollections and that one or more stories may stir your own memories of youthful times and put a smile on your face.

My thanks to my wife Doris, friends and editors Ralph and Jean Pope, as well as Ester Perne and the Summertime News staff for first printing these stories. Many thanks to Bill Pulsifer and Frannie Grant for their photos.

The Pulsifer Boathouse and old Association docks in back of new MLRC building

Boathouses in outer stream shown during extreme low water, probably for dam repair or dredging

Chapter I: The Boathouse

It was a fairly normal day I suppose, probably June something in about 1953. I was fiddling along the shoreline of the stream behind my parent's house, and other owners as well. Main street in Belgrade Lakes was kind of all one then; no one paid much attention to property lines, unless a feud got started over something like a tree or a water line. It was expected or maybe condoned that little kids of 5 years more or less could and would wander about, fishing along the shoreline and exploring everything along the way. They all knew who's kid I was and kept half an eye open in the event my youth got me into trouble. The old saying: it takes a village to raise a child was true then and should be now as far as I'm concerned. That day I had meandered farther than any previous outing and new adventures opened up with every few steps.

The BOATHOUSE looked like an old grey mountain. The new June grass was knee high with a lightly used path showing, winding down from the house to the opening in the back of the boathouse. It seemed odd and scary, there was no door, just a black opening. With fish rod in hand (a stick with string and a rusty small hook) that old man Lee Law had given me earlier in the summer, I slowly proceeded to enter the dark hole. Lee worked for my Dad tending the boat rentals down by the dam, he always helped all us kids with learning how to fish, what to use for bait as well as tactics.

Little by little curiosity was winning over fear as I drew closer to the dark hole, hoping the old man that lived in the house wouldn't see me. I knew he lived there, as I had seen him from a distance mowing the lawn part way down to the boathouse, including the path. He always wore "old man" t-shirts, the kind with straps only on the shoulders. I had also seen him sit in the old lawn chair in the backyard, smoking a cigarette like my Dad did, and drinking something the men call Narry Gansett or sometimes they said Nasty Gansett, and laughed. He sweat like crazy when he mowed and I was a little scared of him. He didn't seem to be around when I stole a couple of secret looks over my shoulder, however, I tumbled over a large metal chunky thing with big pulleys and went down into the high grass face first and hit hard. After reconnoitering, the black hole remained the target and I crept on. Oh, I later learned the metal chunky thing was a make and brake engine, called "one lungers" that powered things like sawmills and boat lifts. The big pulley drove a flat belt. I can tell you now that much or most of the boards that built the older homes on Main Street were sawn with a big rotary blade turned by a one lunger.

My first steps over the threshold into the dark interior made my toes curl. So much to see, fear, like and question. Had it not been for the fact that I was looking out through two huge openings into the stream, I probably would have turned and high tailed it for home. The two boat stalls were empty and as my eyes adjusted to the lack of direct sunlight, everything seemed at least okay, if not friendly. The fear had subsided if not evaporated and without conscious thought the fish line went in the water, dried-on worm and all, testing to see if any red fins were there. They were a type of perch that we kids called a cross between white and yellow perch. They tasted the same as either and in later years we never bothered to differentiate, just cooked them up with the others. In those days, sun fish or sunnies were ever present, ready to steal bait. They were considered not good to eat; we treated them like pests and tossed them back in the pond. I think old man Lee Law had told us they were not worth bothering with.

It wasn't long before I noticed a small corner closet of sorts, with a jammed open door. A metal object that I already knew was an outboard motor was leaning

8

precariously against the interior wall. The redfish got off easy after that as fishing took a hind row seat and I was led to the closet and gawking at the motor, dreams and excitement about its use and potential dancing in my head. Whether 30 seconds or 5 minutes passed, I do not know, but out of the blue came a raspy heavy voice that said: "WHAT ARE YOU DOING IN HERE, SON?" My worst fears nearly cauterized me in place. I slowly looked up to see the old man with the white strap t-shirt just inside the doorway. I must have stuttered a little but I heard myself meekly saying, "I'm fishing."

He said which shocked me beyond words, "DO YOU LIKE THAT OUTBOARD MOTOR?"

I said, "Yes sir" and he said simply "If you can get it running it's yours to use." With that he turned and walked out the door hole and headed back up to the house.

As I stood there happily stunned, he turned back to me and yelled something like : "You'd better head home, your Mom is looking all over town for you." After that, Old Bill Pulsifer was my newest friend. Sometime during the next decade, the men in town tore that boathouse down, along with many others. The pilings, or cribs as we call them, are still visible just underwater on the South side of the new MLRC docks. Young Bill Pulsifer and wife Marie live in the same house today. Don't miss the next installment called—you got it, The Outboard Motor.

THE END

Log Boathouse

Old boathouse in Austin's Bog, recently collapsed.

The old Champion, just like the one from the Pulsifer boathouse

Chapter II: The Outboard Motor

As it turned out, the small outboard tucked away in the boathouse closet was a 4.5 horsepower Champion. It was kind of a silvery color, a little blue paint left here and there. After years of non-use, old grease and motor oil had collected dirt and dust as well as plenty of spider dung. Even the smell of the old oil and dirt coupled with smells of the musty boathouse closet made my excitement level move up a notch or two. The dream of having my own outboard was much closer to being a reality than it had ever been before. Thank You, Old Bill.

The boat I had imagined it powering was about a 10 foot wooden flat bottom scow that Mr. and Mrs. Koref had given my father. Dad was their camp caretaker and they were also close friends. At that time the Korefs owned what is now the Gawler camp on Great Pond. Their youngest boy, Emil, had apparently outgrown the boat. Likely that Mr. K had told Dad to get rid of the boat, either at the dump or in a burn pile. That was the usual demise of old wooden crafts that were no longer needed, or too rotted to float. Instead, Dad had dragged it home the summer before and said I could have it to paddle around down behind the house. Our house was 3 houses South of Old Bill's on the same side of the street, the white square one with a tin roof across from the lime colored house. I had paddled or pushed the scow around as best possible along a hundred feet of shoreline, Mother's assigned boundaries. Other boats were going in and out of the stream powered by outboards, and there were still a few of the old double enders or guide boats going out on occasion. The guide boats had older type gasoline inboard engines and some even had hand cranks to start them. At that time, wooden boats were frowned upon and were a dying breed. Aluminum and fiberglass hulls were starting to take the place of wood, although a short romance

13

with molded plywood hulls came along then too. My Dad bought several plywood hulls from Canada and fitted them with decks, rails and transoms during the winters. The sports liked them and he rented them to seasonal renters that stayed at the Locust House. Unfortunately, the keels and stems were made from birch wood and it rotted quickly. Those plywoods were gone in 15 years, but other brands and material techniques still survive today.

Back to the motor. The looks of the motor as previously described, belied the way it ran. I forget the details of how or who helped me, but the motor became a running reality and it fit nicely on the Koref's old scow. It ran great for at least a couple of summers and probably drove the stream neighbors half crazy, as it only stopped to refuel or to go fishing. Mother's previous boundaries had been stretched to the whole inner stream, from the narrows way down to the bridge. Of course, no boundary is a perfect science and Mother's generous latitudes got cheated on. Whenever she went into town (Waterville) to get groceries, do banking or whatever, my cousin Cary and I would sneak up through the narrows and into Pentlarge Cove. We knew turtles lived there and sunned themselves on the big rocks. Dumont Townsend who lived with Ines Bean, L.L's sister-in-law I think, would give us 25 cents each for every big snapper we could deliver. Talk about capitalism starting early, we were 9 then. Dumont and Ines lived just up the stream, second place in on the left as you enter from the lake, directly across from L.L. Bean's old place where Sid and Julie Dupont live now. Dumont drilled holes in the perimeter of the shell and kept them at his dock on a 20 foot wire leader—until he was ready to make turtle soup.

I don't really remember what became of the old Champion, I think perhaps Dad made me take it back and put it in the boathouse. The motor was now seen as "too small" and we needed something faster. My brother Dick joined the Army in 1956 along with other boys in

14

town. I think perhaps Donald Hanson, Puggy Damren, Tom Sawyer, Stacy Yeaton, Mel Pray and a few others reported to Fort Dix that year. The point is, they left their toys behind and we younger boys scoffed them up. My brother and Frank Megill had both bought new Chris Craft 10 horsepower outboards in 1955 or 1956. Most people today don't know that Chris Craft made outboards, and why should they, unless they were an old motor head. My brother's 10 horsepower Chris Craft became my second engine. Dad gave me a 10 foot plywood hull that didn't rent well due to it's size and the Chris was coupled to it. The unit was a hot item on Great Pond during the summers of '57, '58, and '59. The only thing slightly faster was Dudley Cunningham's canvas covered runabout with a new Johnson 35 horsepower. Dudley is part of the Dowse family that owned the south end of Hoyt's Island prior to the current owners, Bill and Joan Witkin. The newly formed Belgrade Chamber of Commerce (after the hotel burned in 1956) had sponsored a boat race in 1959 and Dud beat me by a boat length. I think Dad and Mom realized they had a maniac on their hands at that point, but Mother held her breath and Dad had a Narry Gansett.

At the age of 11 or 12, my newer summer friend Ralph Pope and I flipped the boat at full speed out in front of his folks camp (Loon Lodge), deep in the cove by the Great Pond Marina. Ralph got whacked on the head by the gunnels when she came over. His brother Larry and Grandpa came out and rescued us as they had been on the dock reading the paper while we were out there raising hell. Ralph's head was bleeding like a stuck pig, but it turned out it was only superficial. Boys will be boys. Ralph's Dad only came up from Boston on weekends, and I think he realized that he needed to step in soon as we boys were having way too much fun; also the gasoline charge at Day's Marina was considerable! In those days, most lake dwellers just drove in to the marina, filled up with gas and signed a little slip of

15

paper. More to come on that.

The exact demise of the Chris Craft 10 is a cloudy memory, but I think that racing and too many dunkings in Great Pond put an end to it. When brother Dick returned from the Army in late 1959 there wasn't much left of that fast motor. I see those motors now in collections and know that once upon a time they went like the wind.

THE END

Other antique outboards: front, 1948 Sea King; back left, 1939 Evinrude; back right, 1923 Johnson

Chapter III: Swimmin' at the Dam (and other places)

Along the same span of years as learning about boats and motors, all of the town kids had been learning to swim.

During the early 1950's, all the mothers of the so-called "war babies" brought their kids to what we called Sandy Beach. The ages of the young ran from new baby to 10 years, more or less. Now we're called the "boomers." Sandy Beach was actually a misnomer, as it was a gravely stretch of shoreline with a couple of wooden docks in the very narrowest part of the stream, where boats can barely pass each other. If you've come into Belgrade Lakes village from Great Pond, you know the place. The place is accessed by a road then called Skunk Alley. It has more polite names, one of which is Red Oaks Lodge Road, no doubt named after the lodge that burned sometime in the 70's after falling into years of disrepair. It sat about where the Zinckgraf place is now.

Each July and August day, weather permitting, the parade of baby carriages and white skinny legged kids would head down the alley to Sandy Beach. The older ones ran then jumped, dove or cannonballed off the dock until lips were blue, and mothers threatened not coming again if they didn't stop. Bombarding passing boats and splashing the occupants with the perfect cannonball was, of course the ultimate. The little ones sat in the gravel wash and made castles or some other creation. Clay that was easily dug out of the gravel make nice artifacts, ash trays were in at that time.

Mothers sat on towels on the lawn just back from the water, keeping one eye on the children while chatting about all the issues of the day. Ken and Eunice Pray owned the property and the big white house up behind it. Ken took pride in keeping it nice for all the towns' people to use.

Ken was also known as Judge Pray, mostly called "Judge," though with no degree in law. Judge was the head grounds keeper at the old Belgrade Hotel that burned in the fall of 1956. He and the summer golf course crew put on large scale lobster bakes down by the shore of Long Pond, where Lakeshore Drive meets the lake. The hotel had a boathouse there at that time. Judge was a huge strong man, and could settle any dispute that might come within the crew, usually without lifting a finger. Judge was a good man with a scythe and taught the older boys in town what a crooked stick was, and made them use it to keep the high grass down on the perimeter of the golf course. Weed wackers had not been invented at that time. He also was boss of what he called the "chain gang shop," where workers gathered in the morning and the mowers were kept.

Other swimming holes took preference as we all got a little older—and free of mother's watchful eyes. The DAM at the end of the stream offered adventurous kids a plethora of potential fun, and risk. On the stream side of the bridge, we, like every generation before and after, began jumping and diving off the bridge. Cannonballs and summersaults put one in an exalted position within the crowd. The crowning achievement praised by all was a wild yelling jump immediately after pulling down your swim trunks and mooning the passing cars. The blowing of a car horn gave even more credence that we had done an entertaining job.

The Long Pond side of the bridge and DAM offered a more interesting swimming area that was either calm pools just below the spillway, or a torrid rapid, depending on how much the dam was open. When interest waned there we moved further out by the point, now the little park, and searched underwater for fishing tackle lost to rocks and other snags. Many people fished there in that era. We used some of what we found, traded some and sold

18

some. Old man Lee Law, who tended Cliff Johnson's boat shop, (which is now Lake Point Realty) would usually give us a quarter for the remaining tangled mess. We would immediately trot across the bridge to Day's Store, previously Bartlett's, where we'd turn the cash into soda pop or ice cream!

THE END

Mothers and kids at Sandy Beach

1930 Woodland Camps swimming beach

Jackson Liberty jumping off bridge

Nice examples of old Stanley Steamers, much like Chester Thwing's

22

Chapter IV: The Stanley Steamer —along with Chester Thwing and Woodland Camps

That old quote that it takes a village to bring up a child must also hold true for a flock of children. Fortunately, the slew of kids of many ages in Belgrade Lakes were somewhat looked after by most of the elders. We roamed the only three streets, not counting the West Road, on foot or bicycles looking for any adventure that might pop up. Of course, there was Main Street, like any town, then School street as we call it today, actually a branch of Skunk Alley. Now Skunk Alley is called by more polite names like Red Oaks Lodge Road, sometimes Hulin Road. For you that don't remember or never knew it, there was a big old Lodge way at the end of the road, about where the Zinckgraf place is, second one outside of the stream. The old Lodge burned one night after falling into much disrepair, I'd guess in the late 70's.

Well, back to it. One of the very special adventures that always drew us up Main Street was the sound of steam escaping, in large amounts, like a high volume sssshhhhh— almost a squeal. We all knew what it was, and the race was on. The noise signaled the fact that Chester Thwing was firing up the Stanley Steamer, which happened once or twice a summer. Chester loved to get the huge vehicle out of the garage and take all the neighborhood kids for a ride. No parental asking or disclaimers signed here, just get in if you could. The Stanley burned kerosene to heat water in the boiler. When it turned to steam, it was directed to turn the rear wheels, similar to a steam train. The Stanley twins produced steam cars from 1902 to 1924 in Newton, Massachusetts.

Chester always wore his cap and duster, even the

goggles. He packed in 8 to 10 of us and off we'd go, heading south down Route 27. We took turns sitting right next to Chester and he let each kid hold the wooden steering wheel. Also, each one took a turn holding the lever on the column which controlled the steam power to the wheels. We'd all scream when Wayne French, who lived on School Street, would have his turn. Wayne would promise dutifully not to pull the lever way down to fast, but he did it anyway and mayhem would break out. The screaming got even louder and Chester would feign getting Wayne's hand off the lever, and by that time we were going like hell.

By the time we were part way to the Depot, we'd used a lot of steam and water. Chester would pull over at Bog Brook. He kept about a dozen thick 6 ounce Coke bottles on the trunk shelf and put us in a brigade to bring him water from the brook. He'd fill the water tank until the sight glass showed pretty much full. Soon, he'd yell, "All Aboard" like a train conductor, then quickly repack the bottles as we bailed back in, always fighting for the wheel spot beside Chester. After reaching the Depot, he'd usually hit the West Road down by the tracks and come back that way.

As he pulled back into his yard and brought the Steamer to a halt, we'd bail out again and head off to find the next adventure, while yelling our thanks and asking when we could go again.

Chester was a man of many talents and much ambition. He built Woodland Camps on Great Pond right around 1920. The Lodge and 16 cabins were built over several years. The hemlock trees provided the framing 2x4's and 2x6's and the same trees provided the bark covered slabs for siding. It is likely that the trees were taken across the two coves on the ice, sawed at Dalton's saw mill, then returned before ice out. Dalton's sawmill sat right about where the Community Center is now. In the 1950s, there was still a huge pile of sawdust there. Horses or oxen and

24

sleds were likely used to transport the lumber both ways. Some 90 years later much of the bark siding still shows on the cabins. The cabins all exist today, as modified. One burned in May of 1985 but was quickly rebuilt before July. Chester had a brother that built like-kind cabins on the north end of Hoyt's Island during the same era. Old hearsay has it that they squabbled over something, parted company and each built their own set of cabins.

When Chester Thwing died, he left the camps to his son-in-law Don Mosher. After a few years Don sold the place to Clayton and Betty Grant. Clayton died in 1982 and Betty ran it alone with hired help and friends for 2 or 3 years. After her retirement about 1986, she sold the units to individual owners with business partners Jim Williams and Darryl Day.

Oh, forgot this. Not too long after Chester died, we kids gathered on his front lawn and silently watched as a big flatbed truck took the steamer away. We never saw it again and thought that life had changed forever—it did mark the end of an era for us. The good news is you can see one like it. Go to the Stanley Museum in Kingfield, Maine.

THE END

p.s. Stanley Museum ph. # is: 207-265-2729   or Maine@StanleyMuseum.org
p.p.s. The museum also has many portraits as well as antique violins

"Pine Beach Camp" Great Lake, Belgrade Lakes, Me.

Typical rental boats delivered to camps

The old boat shop where Ernest Solar, Ralph Stuart, and Cliff Johnson built guide boats and Rangely type rental boats. The site is where Lake-point Realty is now. The shop burned in 1972.

Chapter V: Deliverin' Boats on Great Pond

I'm guessing it was the summer of 1957. The Champion 4.5 horsepower on the flat-bottomed scow was plying the stream all the way out to the lake. Once past the narrows Mother couldn't see us, so the sky was the limit.

Dad was working on convincing Mother that it would probably be okay to let me run a boat all the way to Bear Spring Camps, while towing several others. Mother was a sport, but this must have stretched her good will to the limit. She finally agreed, but told Dad that the first trip could only be to Woodland Camps, about one third as far, with less chance of getting lost.

Our boat rental business down by the dam, where Lake Point Realty is now, did daily rentals to fisherman from the local area, but also supplemented the boat needs of several sets of cabins. Most cabins had some boats, but never enough if all the cabins were full and the sports all wanted boats. When a call came in from places like Bear Springs, Woodland, Joyce's Island, or even Clement's Camps on Long Pond, the boats had to be delivered. The boats were the old wooden lapstrakes, commonly know as Rangley boats, but these were built right here in Belgrade Lakes by father's predecessors, Ralph Stuart and Ernest Soler, both having passed away. We had a few molded plywoods that some people preferred, they were wider and deeper.

Being that older brother Richard had joined the Army and was in Bordeaux, France, my chance to be the delivery captain came to fruition. Dad would fit his newest 5 horsepower Johnson (the one with the neutral lever on top) onto the first boat, then hook from 2 to 4 others together with short painters, creating the fleet. He'd say go ahead, I'll meet you there. The excitement turned to uneasy feelings and then light fear after leaving the familiar waters of the stream and heading to my vague destination. He'd mumbled, with evidence of Red Top snuff on his lips, something like: "head out past the first point, give it a wide berth 'cause there's a bunch of big rocks in close, then head about 2 o'clock and you'll see the big flag." Well, considering the fleet was only moving about 2 mph, getting lost or found was going to take some time. The directions were good enough and the flag did in fact appear, although there was some skepticism as to whether it was the correct one.

Finally, arriving near shore by the flag and seeing other green Rangleys at several docks, my confidence reappeared. Slowly rounding the breakwater in front of Woodland Camps, I killed the 5 Johnson when hearing some yelling. Sure enough, there was Dad and Don Mosher, sitting in rockers up on the Lodge porch having a so-called "toddy." Mission accomplished, Don gave me a soda. We took the 5 Johnson off the boat, threw it the back of the pickup and reported home to Mother that it was "no big deal."

Later in the summer, there were other opportunities to deliver. The big one came in early August when the cabins around the lake were all overflowing with sports. Margarete Mosher from Bear Spring Camps called and wanted 4 boats as soon as we could get them up there. Dad rigged them up to tow after work and I got some vague directions, but had never been in that part of the lake. I think he said "cross the same point as if going to Woodland, only keep your course through the gut (south end of Hoyt's and Long Point) and keep the big rocks sticking out of the water (the white ledges) on your right. Again, look for a flag on a point (Jamaica Point) and go through that narrows, keep the land close on your left and follow way down into the cove. You'll see the cabins on the big sand beach." After what seems like an ocean crossing, perhaps with celestial guidance, the beach and cabins did appear. Dad and Bert

Mosher (I don't think Don and Bert were related) were sitting on a tiny cabin porch having a "toddy."

THE END

1948 postcard of Woodland Camp shore in the early days

Charlie Grant and his guide boat

Cliff Johnson and helper bailing rental boats after a rainstorm

Chapter VI: Guide Boats

During the 20th century, the economy of the greater Belgrade area was partially, if not primarily, driven by tourist's dollars. This included the Lakes, the Depot and North Belgrade, as well as the entire watershed of the seven lake chain. Many sets of "fishing cabins" housed summer folk, but when 1900 rolled around, several larger hotels became available. Places like The Belgrade Hotel, Lakeshore Hotel, The Locust House and others came into vogue. The train came into the Depot so "Folks From Away" came in greater numbers, and it took greater numbers to care for them. Of the many drawing cards of our area, such as the beauty and quiet, there was FISHIN. In those early days, the number and size of the fish were beyond today's imagination. Many pictures of large catches were recorded and reside in our history books.

Many of the local men became guides who were hired to take sports fishing. The demand for a good number of boats to ply the waters of the Belgrade chain fostered the building of what became known as guide boats. These boats varied in size from 18 to 26 feet, were pointed on both ends, like a canoe. They were powered by 1 to 4 cylinder gasoline engines that sat amidships. The early models had to be hand cranked like a Model T Ford, the electric starters came along later.

The guide boats were fitted with at least two comfy chairs for the sports, including arm and backrests. The guide sat near the motor and could row from there, or from the front chair, if only one sport was aboard. Most boats had no reverse, so oars were used to back her out and head her out. Most trolling was done by oar as well, as the old motors could not idle slow enough to suit the trout and salmon. See the 1976 history book for pictures of these boats, as well as the pictures included here, courtesy of Bill

Pulsifer and Franny Grant.

Many, if not most, of the guide boats built in Belgrade were built in the boathouse that sat where Lake Point Realty sits now. Ernest Solar and Ralph Stuart were the primary builders up into the 1950's. My Dad, Cliff Johnson, a student of Ralph's, carried on repairing the existing boats until little demand remained. The building, as well as the boat patterns, was razed in a bonfire c. 1972. A few of these boats have survived through philanthropy and museum help. Joe Tinker has presented one in the last several boat parades on July Fourth. That is the same boat that is shown in the 1976 Bicentennial Book, with Everett Johnson and Bunny Tillson aboard. I believe that boat came from the August Family Camp on Indian Island, Great Pond.

Many if not most guide boats were winter stored in the many boathouses that lined the stream leading from Great Pond to the dam in Belgrade Lakes. Each spring, part of the ritual of getting the boats ready to use, required letting them "swell up." Being made of all wood and most single planked, the boats dried out during the winter and the seams opened up. Most guides initially lowered the boats only partially into the water via chain falls or rope block and tackle. The boats would immediately leak partially full, but being suspended by the falls, could not sink. After a few days the boats were bailed out and released to float upon their own. In many instances, large cracks or openings in the planks were chinked with cotton rope, oakum, and or white lead, then painted prior to dunking.

The engines could be temperamental, but each guide got to know the tricks to start his boat quite easily, usually with a few cranks. Priming cups were necessary for a cold start. These were mounted on top of the cylinder head, were about the size of a thimble, and a small amount of gasoline was put in each one. A small valve was opened just prior to cranking, allowing the fuel down into the combustion chambers. Remember, the boat had to be positioned

32

seaward. The older ones had no neutral or reverse, so were immediately propelled forward when the engine fired up.

THE END

Association docks with guide boats

Intrigued with photographer's gadgets are, left to right: unknown photographer, Mr. Bean, Everett Johnson, and Charles Grant

Charlie Grant at Watson Pond with fox, 1924

Chapter VII: The Guides

Some of the old guides who come to mind were still alive when I was a young boy, hanging out in the boat shop and running up and down the stream with the 4.5 Champion. I feel very fortunate to have known them, as they were a dying breed and every one a character in himself. The names that come to mind, and no disrespect to the others that I did not know, are: Fred Ellis, Wilkie Collins, Charlie Grant, Everett and Ernest Johnson, Russell Morrell. Others shown in the photo supplied by Bill Pulsifer are Ed Austin, Leon Farnham, Merle Rix, Charlie Hulen, Ed Megill, and Charlie Brown.

Guides duties included supplying a properly fitted boat and equipment to take person or persons out to catch fish, probably in some reasonable form of comfort. Also, teaching fishing tactics, being astute enough to know when they needed assistance, and when to leave them to the fishing. Guides also offered a mid-day break, which included a picnic stop with lunch served. The lunches might include fried perch over an open fire, fish chowder made the night before and reheated, or more simple lunches put up by the kitchen staff of the hotels. The guides had several established spots with rock fire pits and a rustic table. As a young kid I had visited "under the mountain" and a couple on Hoyt's Island. Old man Lee Law, an avid fisherman who tended the boat shop for Dad, along with Elmer Green who ran Gilman's Camps (North side of the Dam) taught me to fish and where the lunch places were. They also let me drive the boat. We caught big salmon on sewed-on bait, which were red fish (perch) that I had caught in the steam. They skinned the little fish and sewed them onto wire leaders with fine copper braid, double hooks out the belly, with a slight curve to make it wiggle while being trolled. Both Lee and Elmer had "sips" out of the whiskey bottle as the day wore on. They both sat back with large smiles on their faces as I turned the final corner into the stream, usually by mid-afternoon. Elmer rolled his own smokes with Prince Albert pipe tobacco, and probably died from it. I never realized until many years later that actually I had taken them fishing, not the other way around. It was a win-win for both sides. I think I learned 80% of what I know today from guys like old Elmer Green and Lee Law.

Fred Ellis: Fred was a character who plied the sidewalks of Belgrade Lakes for many years. Fred lived in a rustic house on Skunk Alley, actually named Hulin Road and sometimes referred to as Red Oaks Lodge Road. His house was two houses past where Parker Johnson lives now. The fire department burned Fred's house after he died. In his elder years when I remember him, he no longer guided, but his boat rested on crossbeams in a boathouse behind the Village Inn, later torn down. His daily routine was to walk up the alley with his dog, pushing a wheelbarrow. He would go to the post office, then in the middle of the village, and pick up the mail for Day's Store. He faithfully brought the mail daily and was paid with two bottles of Dawson Ale, an arrangement made by Fred and Jim (Grampa) Day. Fred would leave the store with his pay and proceed to the boathouse across from what was then Russell Morrell's house, now Don RyCroft and Carol Johnson's place. He would have his morning beer and leave the second on the shelf for the afternoon pilgrimage. I only know this because we local boys would swim and fish in the boathouse and on occasion had a sip to see what it tasted like. One of Fred's last deeds was to give me his old guide boat. Father Clifford asked what in H___ I intended to do with it, and of course I had no idea. It stayed at the boat rental docks for a couple of weeks, constantly trying to sink. My knuckles were raw from cranking it and it never did run. Old Windy Earl Moulton from Rome Hollow stopped in to talk shop with Dad every other week or so
36

and offered me $25 for it. I thought I'd retire early and took it. He towed it up to Rome and I never saw it again. Dad said it served him right. Fred got older and more sick and was taken to Togus Veteran's Hospital, where he was cared for until his death. He was a WW 1 veteran.

Wilkie Collins: In the mid 1950s, Wilkie was quite an old and decrepit man. He wiled away many hours sitting at the boat rental shop and chatting with whoever might show up. Dad called him and others "sidewalk superintendents." Wilkie braided all the anchor rode to the ring anchors, his hands were big and knarled. Bunny Tillson said he had been a cable splicer in the Navy during WW1 and that arthritis had settled in badly. When Wilkie died, his old 36 Ford sedan was still in the boatshop driveway. It sat there for a year or so and I think Dad had Bud Knowles tow it to the junkyard.

Charlie Grant: Had 4 sons, Henry, Harry, Jessie and Albert, and one daughter Lottie. He always wore knickers and a campaign hat, also small dark glasses. He would occasionally guide in the early 50's, but often just visited and puttered on his boat. There were many old docks called the Association Docks, more or less where the LRC docks are now. Charlie shot a deer at the age of 96, the last year he was alive. His son Harry would help or carry him to his favorite apple orchard just before dusk and lean him up against his favorite apple tree to wait for a deer. Franny Dill Grant is his granddaughter.

Everett Johnson: Guided some, hunter, trapper, built and ran the marina just across from Day's Store. Had two sons, Karl and Byron. Plowed the town roads for years with a big orange FWD equipped with a huge V-plow and two wings. He last resided with wife Harriett in what is now the Witkin's village house, just across from Day's. Was caretaker of Hoyt's Island south end camp for several generations including tenures of the Mitchells and the Dowses.

Ernest Johnson: My paternal grandfather, guide, hunter and trapper, camp caretaker, father of three boys: Clifford, Walter, and Albert. His wife and the boy's mother was Alice Cummings. They lived on School Street where David and Kris Veins live now. He died while tending mink traps in lower Long Pond in 1952.

Russell Morrell: Guide, excellent fisherman. Lived in the house (now being renovated) just North of Day's Store right beside the dam, most recently purchased by Donald RyCroft and Carol Johnson. When the perch were running down at the dam, lots of people fished for them. Russell would wait patiently for an open spot where the worm dunkers were fishing, step in with a grey ghost on a fly rod and pluck out the big humpbacks.

Ed Megill: Business owner and also good guide and fisherman. Owned and ran the Manor and the Locust House (now the Village Inn). Knew a lot of things and could do most of them.

I'm sure there's lots more to tell about the guides, and as we find it out we'll put together another segment and pass it along. Hail to the GUIDES.

An assembly of area guides in the Locust House, now The Village Inn. Back row, L-R: Merle Rix, Ed Megill, Leon Farnham, Russell Morrill, and Charlie Brown. Front Row: L-R: Charlie Hulin, Ed Austin, Fred Ellis, Wilkie Collins, and Charlie Grant (1947).

Charlie Grant at age 96. See story next page.

Retired Guide Charlie Grant, 96 Will 'Try A Shot Or Two' This Fall

By PAULINE PLOURDE

BELGRADE LAKES — Charles Russell Grant was 96 years old in September, only six years past his last guiding trip here on Great Pond.

A squall came up that day in 1961 and drove his boat onto a rock and stove it up. The man and woman with him weren't hurt, but losing that boat helped Grant decide that his 45 years of guiding hereabouts, and to the north, were about finished.

Grant was born on Bridge street in Augusta, son of Leonard and Lydia French Grant. He had one sister and three brothers, but has outlasted them all.

He remembers his first job, for a harness shop near the old bridge. Then he worked for the Capitol Case Co., later for the Parker Truck firm in Bangor.

For a good many springs he was on the log drives of the Guilford Lumber Co., working the Piscataquis River and neighboring streams.

BUT FISHING has been the best part of his many years. "Thirty years ago you could catch 444 bass in six days, put them all back and still feel it was good sport", he says. "Now a man who catches a dozen bass on a fly thinks he's lucky."

Guides were a help in letting fishermen really find the fish, he thinks. "I remember when we had 55 guides right here in Belgrade. It was hard work, especially when you had to handle a canoe in wind, but the fishing was good."

Charles Grant makes his home with his son, Harry F. Grant, who also has guided.

However, Harry Grant leans more toward the hunting, and has done safety instructing for the National Rifle Assn. for many years.

"When the lake water used to be held at a certain level, the fish had a better chance," the younger Grant remarks. "Now the level is dropped, ice freezes to the bottom, no air can get under it and the spawns freeze up."

Both men feel that reclaiming ponds has drawbacks. "When they kill everything out of a pond, there's no food left for the trout and salmon they stock it with, so the new fish have to eat each other," Harry Grant says.

Charlie Grant likes to have his family call, and many of them were with him for a pre-birthday celebration.

His daughter, Mrs. Lottie Boynton of South China, his sons, Henry Grant of Belgrade Lakes and Jesse Grant of Rome, and Jesse Grant's wife, were there. Mrs. Charles Grant died many years ago. She had been Ida Ella Hezelton of Lynn, Mass.

Also present were grandchildren; Harold Grant, Augusta, Mrs. Maple Tracy, South China, and Mr. and Mrs. Vernon Boynton and their three children.

Won't they be surprised if he gets a deer this fall? "I'll try a shot or two," Charlie promises.

Bobwhite quail have an annual mortality rate of about 80 per cent whether they are hunted or not.

Chapter VIII: Goin' up to the Farm

Most every Sunday we had to go up to the farm. My Mom's folks, Henry and Blanche Parlin, lived and farmed on Route 27. It was 8 miles north of the Lakes, just back from Route 2, where the turkey farm is now. Usually Dad couldn't go as he tended the boat rentals himself on Sundays, old man Lee Law needed a day off to go fishing.

Mother drove the old Buick with me and at least one other kid. Being pulled out of the swimming hole or from catching red fins along the stream shore seemed like punishment. The farm was hot and smelly with flies buzzing around the animals. Our whining was replaced with mischievous thoughts when mother pulled the Buick up the long farm driveway and threw the dynaflow transmission up into park. That was the first car we had that wasn't stick shift.

Grampa usually appeared from the barn or woodshed, probably dreading our visit, knowing from past experience that we'd cause a ruckus. He knew that we liked to torment the animals and often had cow flap (dung piles) fights. Other misdemeanors, like sliding down the manure pile were commonplace. Grampa's one strict order was DO NOT go up in the haylofts, something about packing it down, heat, mildew, fire. The minute he left the barn to go visit Mom and Grammy in the kitchen, we'd head up to the loft to romp in the hay. Every now and then we'd hit a hard spot in the hay, which turned out to be empty Kruger Ale bottles. I later learned that Grammy was a teetotaler, so Grampa winged his empties up into the loft so she wouldn't find them. We found his stash of full Krugers in the milk cooler, behind the big silver cans.

It wasn't long before Gramps was back to check on us. We'd hear his footsteps as he came through the long woodshed between the house and barn. He'd wander and yell for us as we lay super still up in the loft. I'm sure we didn't fool him at all, but he'd give up and go back in. Then it was time to raid Gram's hen house. The chickens would go spastic as we'd disturb them and take the eggs, only to throw them at the cows, either in the field grazing or tied in their stalls.

After aggravating all the animals, it was time for chewing tobacco. Gramps had a stash of "Day's Work" on the window sill in the grain room. It was small rectangular "plugs" about the size of a brownie, individually wrapped in paper. We'd bet on who could keep a mouthful in the longest. Inevitably, one kid would gag and we'd spit up all over the place. In later teenage years, an old timer Carroll Gordon, alias Cabbage from New Sharon, told me that you had to be quite old to chew Days Work. His words were: "I'm 66 and I'm not old enough yet". This from a man who chewed Red Top or Copanhagen snuff most waking hours. Cabbage was a relative of the Day family and worked at Day's Marina in the 60's. He was one of our folk heroes, right up there with Lee Law, Red Buzzell and others.

Some Sundays were special and we went up early to prepare and eat "dinnah." This meant Gram sent Gramp out to cull out a chicken that she called by name, which no longer laid eggs enough to suit her. God forbid that he got the wrong one. We kids were sent to help (watch) as he killed the chicken and "dressed it out." It took place in the cow barn and was a gory detail. I think we kids learned right there that chickens didn't come from Shaw's Market without some previous preparation. When it was done we proudly followed Gramp back into the kitchen with carcass in hand, ready for the boiling pot that Gram and Mother had going. Of course, it was 95 degrees in the kitchen some days, as the big old Glenwood had to be fired up to cook the chicken. The farm had wood heat only, and minimum electricity. Water came by using the hand pump on the sideboard by the soapstone sink.

By late afternoon, mother had cleaned us up from the cow manure battles. She put old towels on the back seat of the Buick and headed back to the lake! Yeah.

Socializing in the barnyard

Parlin Farm in New Sharon

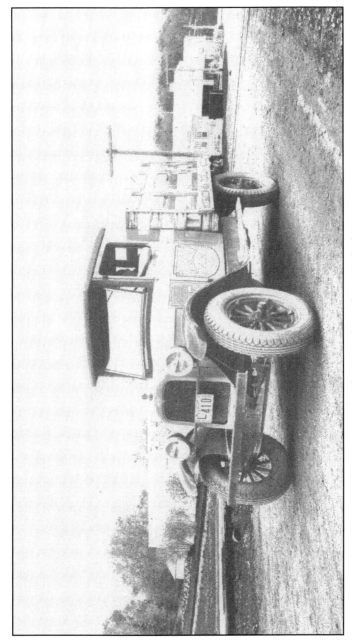

1926 Chevy truck similar to Pukin' Betsy

Chapter IX: Pukin' Betsy

This should be part of a chapter not yet written, called Scooters, Motorbikes, and Cars, or something similar, outlining the life of motor head kids in the 50's and 60's. Problem one is, the story of this car deserves a chapter of its own. Problem two is, none of we kids could figure out how to spell PUKIN', you know as in throw up, heave your innards. In our thinking and Maine lingo, that's the best we could do. So it was, the car was named PUKIN' BETSY. The day Fred Saxton first got it fired up in the yard, one of the old timers, either Cabbage or Red, said the name and we all nodded approvals. The three inch boat letters were applied on both sides of 1926 Chevy's cut down hood, a clear proclamation that we weren't changing our minds.

The story actually started one evening in Barney Durrell's garage yard, located on the shore of Clearwater lake, Industry, Maine. Darryl Day, owner of Day's Marina in Belgrade Lakes, along with bargain Rafe and me as his assistants, were delivering a new 1962 40 horsepower Johnson electramatic-shift outboard. The purchaser was a lake camp owner and Barney was their agent, a common arrangement in those days. Darryl sold several boats and motors to Barney's customers in the 60's and 70's.

Often the deliveries took place after normal working hours, when the marina in the Lakes, across from Day's Store, was either closed for the day, or Darryl's wife Linda would tend the early evening hours. In those days a lot of people came in to get boat gas, drop off a broken motor, and of course, hit the store for some beer or ice cream, maybe even a steak.

Perhaps Barney had bad gout, or maybe he was injured in WWII, that rings a bell. At any rate, his ankles were bad and when we pulled in that evening, Barney came slowly shuffling out of the back office area. He wore slippers as usual, with about one third of a cigar sticking out of the corner of his mouth. Darryl and Barney went back into the office to tidy up the paperwork, and perhaps to have a "small snifter" to consummate the deal. I think it was actually my Uncle Byron that coined the small snifter phrase, which always has a nice ring to it. Being too young to have any of the so called "brown stuff," Rafe and I stayed outside gawking around, and soon our eyes rested on an old car across the street. Barney had what he called a parking lot, and to be fair it was that, however, often muddy with potholes that would swallow a dog. Almost instantly, visions of having that vehicle were swimming around in our 16 year old heads.

No sooner had that happened when Darryl and Barney appeared, shuffling over to the parking lot. Barney was no fool, and he soon allowed that the car could be available for the right price. I blurted out to Darryl that I'd pay half of whatever the price was. After some haggling, the two elders agreed that the old Scott-Atwater outboard motor that had just been a trade-in, was worth the same as the car. By then, Barney's cigar was just a minor stub and he seemed to be rolling it around, almost like chewing tobacco. The deal was done. Barney kept the old Scott 40 horsepower to resell and we agreed to come back another night to get the 26 Chevy. On the way home Darryl said that he was pleased, as the old Scott was probably junk anyway.

Two nights later, Darryl, Fred Saxton, Rafe, and I headed for Industry. We were driving the Pink Pig, another named vehicle, actually Darryl's '57 Pontiac Chieftain. We used the car like a truck, and were towing a twin-axle flat bed trailer, normally used to launch the larger storage boats into Great Pond. Barney helped us load the flat-tired '26 Chevy onto the trailer, chewing away on a new cigar as he manipulated the levers of his old wrecker truck winch. After some parting "snifters" back in the office, dark had come. Barney then suggested a shortcut back to New

46

Sharon via the Weeks Mills Road, but it did require going through some farm roads to make it work. I was elected to drive as the elders were somewhat inebriated, though in practice we usually swapped off now and then. While working our way through a very rough road, the lights failed on the Pig. We tried going without lights and nearly ran into a cow in the field. Fred, mechanic extraordinaire, and one of the world's best tinkerers, fixed the blown headlight fuse by wrapping it with foil from a gum wrapper. Nice trick, Bucko (one of Fred's many nicknames). After some time, we came out onto Route 2 in New Sharon, and then dusted the Pig still towing its load, down Route 27 to the Lakes, new home of the '26 Chevy.

The next morning, the outboard shop had its usual backlog of broken outboard motors to fix, as well as miscellaneous deliveries and pickups on Great or Long Pond. Boss Darryl said hands off the '26 until all the work was done. Fortunately, Fred showed up from Beaver Cove around noon. Fred and Grace were still summer folks at that time, becoming full time Mainers in the early 1970s. Fred couldn't keep his hands off the old Chevy, and was the perfect man for the job, having a Model A Ford back at camp that he tinkered off and on. By late afternoon, with all of us having snuck a peek now and again, Fred had the '26 Chevy idling out behind the shop, chuk-a-bluck, chuk-a-bluck, and chuk-a-bluck. Now do you think we gave the car the right name?

Within a few days and many cans of Evinrude blue and Johnson red spray paint, the 1926 Chevrolet was a thing of beauty. The old rotted wooden spoke wheels were replaced with Model A Ford wire wheels (thanks Fred) and she was good to go. Bargain Rafe, alias Ralph Pope, a co-conspirator in the fix-up and use of the buggy, and summer employee of the marina, hung huge Chianti wine bottles on the windshield corner posts, instead of wasting a bottle of champagne. The car was a summer mainstay around the

47

Lakes for a couple of summers. I remember picking up my date, Randy Curtain, for the Friday night rec-center dance with the car. When I knocked on the camp door, her mother answered, looked over my shoulder into the driveway and said "what in hell is that," then asked if she could go along.

Here's a fact that readers may appreciate. This 87 year old automobile, wherever it might be, is believed to be the first car ever to get to the top of Smith Hill, where the golf course clubhouse is. In the summer of '63, Ralph Pope, Hunt Dowse, The '26 Chevy and I camped out under the apple tree, right near where the putting green is now. At that time there were no roads going all the way up there, so we picked our way through the woods for the last assault. We had to climb trees to see either lake. Soon after that, Ken Bartlett put in a small road and built a house there, now part of the clubhouse.

Oh yah, an afterthought. The Model A that Fred tinkered at camp is the one that you see in the July 4th parade, now nicely restored by his granddaughter Darryl and her friend Bob. Fred would be proud to see it in today's condition. He and Grace drove that car up here from New Jersey in 1950.

The fate of the '26 Chevy got lost in time, but we ARE looking for it!

THE END

Chapter X:
The Magic of Bean Hole Suppers

Bean hole suppers are nothing new in Belgrade, or in many other Maine towns for that matter. If you stay home and have beans and hot dogs for supper, you generally wouldn't think of that as a gourmet meal. So, why is it that bean hole suppers are called "special"?

Let's start with tradition. Bean hole suppers have Maine written all over them. We may not have been the first to practice cooking beans this way, but we have hung to it pretty well. The Maine logging camps had bean hole beans going almost constantly for 2 centuries. So there, beat that. In the working lumber camps, the beans were a way to feed lots of hungry men for a long winter, as the beans stored well in dry tins, plus they were cheap and plentiful in the summers. Now in our time, bean hole suppers at community gatherings and fund raisers give us a taste of the past in more ways than one.

Belgrade got its start about 1960 when Lyle Strickland, a Belgrade native, went to a bean hole supper in a small town near Winthrop. Lyle returned and came to an ad hoc meeting of the fledging Belgrade Chamber of Commerce. He shared his excitement about the possibilities of starting the bean hole bean tradition as the centerpiece of fund raisers to support the new (under construction then) Belgrade Recreation Center. The early Chamber of Commerce membership included Uncle Al and Aunt Lydia Johnson, Clayton Grant, Bud and Marilyn Young, Ken Bartlett and many others, all of whom agreed to give it a shot and try to put on a bean hole supper. Finding enough black cast iron pots as well as digging and lining a fire pit were first on the list. Pots were acquired hither and skither, one at a time. The back parking lot of the building-in-progress recreation center was the natural choice for the fire pit to be dug. Many volunteers came forth to help dig and line the inside of the pit with large rocks; the rocks primary purpose was to hold the heat after a fire was burned out, though it also kept the pit sides from caving in.

The first fire, set off about noon of the previous day of serving the first Belgrade beans, went off about as planned. The wood was "hardwood slabs" including oak, maple, ash and beech, as prescribed, the best for making coals. Softwood such as pine, hemlock and spruce were no-no's, as they burned up into ash. Most lumber mills, including Hammond's, still had slabs in big bundles before the days of chipping any waste. For folks from away who don't know what slabs are, they are the rounded part of a tree that is sliced off first by the saw mill in order to "square-up" the tree for cutting into boards. Getting the cast iron pots onto the coals, now filled with beans, water and "special flavorings" was no easy task. Oh, incidentally, Al and Lydia Johnson were the keepers of the FLAVORING SECRETS for about the next 25 years, when the torch was passed to Dave and Kris Viens. Uncle Al was often accused of dribbling tobacco juice into the brew.

Moving on: Two men on opposite sides of the long narrow pit held a long pipe and slowly lowered each pot into just the right spot on the bed of coals, the spot having been prepared like a bird's nest by using long shovels or so-called spoons. This nest making business was a very hot task and usually men were sprayed constantly with the water hose. On occasion even the fire truck hose got used. In the early years, only 6 or 8 pots were used, but as more and more people came to the suppers more pots were acquired and the pit was made longer. Currently there are 13 pots used and 120 pounds dry weight of beans cooked, half pea bean and half yellow eye.

The beans cook overnight and are dug up around 6 a.m. Water is usually added and the decision is made to either reset the pot for more cooking or leave it up to stay warm until serving time at 5 p.m. As the years have passed, the volunteers have changed and much knowledge has been passed down. The fire department does a great job now. Many goof-ups happened during the early years and here's just a few of them.

Goof-up #1: We started the fire too early and ran short of wood. We called Skip Hammond and he showed up with the GMC pulp truck loaded with 3 cords of hardwood slabs. Skip hollered "Where do you want it?" Uncle Karl Johnson said "On the fire." So it was, it all went on at once, made an inferno for hours and we couldn't put the beans on the coals until midnight.

Goof-up #2: One year, just after lowering the last pot and covering them all with a topping of hot coals, we got a deluge of rain. A real heavy wham-banger hit us first, and then it settled in and rained all night. We scurried and got some old tin sheets from Donnie Hammond at midnight, but it was a day late and dollar short. The coals got doused down real deep and the next morning at the 6 a.m. dig-up time, we sadly found that no beans were cooked at all. Chairman Karl said, "No problem, put them all in the back of my pickup." We did so and went door to door in Belgrade and Rome, asking to use people's smaller pots and ovens. Everyone said, "Sure, c'mon in." By the time we had them all in ovens it was noon. We re-collected at 3 to 4 p.m. and took the now-cooked beans back to the recreation center pit. While John and Ellen Gawler were a-twangin'-and-a-wailin' away, keeping people very happy, we smuggled the beans back into the big black pots and walked them down to hang on the serving tripods, just at 5 p.m. No one knew the difference and fun was had by all. That's no baloney!

Goof-up #3: Each year a "bean hole chairperson" was elected (even under protest). A summer resident named Pat Murphy agreed to do the job, after all, he ran a business in Virginia and was a good organizer. Well, the day prior to the supper several of us had agreed to meet Pat at the fire pit around noon. We knocked off camp work a bit early and went to the pit to look things over, lay out the tools needed, etc. At 12 o'clock sharp Pat rolled in with his big old Mercedes S 430. We all knew Pat and Carol well so anything could be said. When Pat got out of the car, Mel Pray quickly said, "Where's the beer?" Pat thought he was kidding, but none of us had told Pat that it was the Chairperson's job to bring enough beer to build a fire and keep it burning for several hours. Being a good sport, Pat went down to Day's store and filled the big Mercedes' trunk full of beer and ice. When he returned and opened the trunk for proof, Mel grabbed a beer and went over and lit the fire. The moral of the story in those days was: no beer, no fire.

Goof-up #4: Sometimes the beans were only partially cooked at 6 a.m. One time Bill P., after examining and tasting from a pot, said: "These are not done, I've got an idea and will be right back." He soon returned with wife Marie's hair dryer, for which we jimmied a cord from the water pump circuit and began blowing on the coals with the dryer. It worked great, an electric bellows of sorts. Of course, it's now 7 a.m. and Bill takes the hair dryer home and quietly puts it back on Marie's vanity. After her shower, Marie started to dry her hair. She was instantly sprayed with ashes that had been sucked into the intake of the dryer. Bill was in the dog house for a couple of weeks.

Come one, come all and get your BEANHOLE BEANS. Hats off to all those who have made this annual event possible, both now and in the past.

THE END

Pork n Beans

Beanhole

1939 Dodge pumper when new

Belgrade engine 64 tanker when new

Chapter XI
The Belgrade Cellar Savers

There is no doubt that the Belgrade Fire Department has changed a lot in just 50 years. Today's armada of modern fire trucks and trained volunteers do a great job of protecting property, limiting damage and reducing loss of life.

Let's go back to about 1960 and see what it was like in this small town with three villages and many rural houses. As is true now, each village had a firehouse or garage of some caliber, and each had a truck with a small amount of equipment. At that time the Depot sported a 1952 Chevy pumper, North Belgrade had a 1946 Dodge and the Lakes had a 1939 Dodge open cab. The volunteer departments were loosely formed by whoever showed up. To my knowledge there was not so much as a written list naming anyone in particular as a member, people just came if they could or felt like it. This soon changed and by the mid to latter 1960's, names were taken down at the station after the fire and memberships developed.

During the same late 60's period, Bill Pulsifer (Chief at large and overall spokesman), was making an annual pilgrimage to the March town meetings. He always spoke well and presented the need for updated equipment and the funds to finance it. Often there were a few mumblings amongst some of the elders that thought we were just fine with what we had, but when Town Moderator Clyde Bickford dropped the gavel and asked for a show of hands, Bill's requests for decent-sized chunks of money were almost always granted. Reserve funds were built and the first brand new fire truck in many years was spec'd out and ordered. In 1963, several of the local boys (namely Bill Pulsifer, his father Bill, Calvin Hanson, Dick Johnson and Clayton Grant) went to Massachusetts to the Farrar factory and drove the 1963 GMC pumper to its new home in

Belgrade Lakes. Upon hitting the Belgrade town line down below the Depot, they blew the siren all the way to the Lakes and had a large following of cars and trucks when they arrived home. Some people were a little peeved at the false alarm, but soon got over it after seeing the truck. Around 1970, North Belgrade got a big GMC 750 gpm (gallons per minute) pump truck. Belgrade Depot's '52 was retired some years later, having been replaced by another new 1000 gpm General Motors truck.

As you can imagine, with little organization or training and very poor communications, more often than not follies happened. At that time, the fire alert was a siren usually mounted on the firehouse roof, with an on off switch inside the building. A call to report a fire and ask for help came into public places like the general store or saw mill or post offices. For a decade or so, a red phone system (actually colored red—you know, like the president has) was installed in the aforementioned places. Whoever took the call would yell to whoever was free to go the station and turn on the siren, then return to work. All well and good, men would be seen running to get to the fire truck, pickups slewing into the firehouse driveways. Rivalries as to who got there first did exist, although they were not talked about much. At night, partially dressed men would jump into the truck and take off. Turn out gear was minimal and optional, though someone might throw on a raincoat or boots if it was cold outside. The largest folly was that often no one who had reached the firehouse knew where the fire was and the truck couldn't take off until someone showed up that knew. Dah! After that a chalkboard was put up for the turn-on-person to jot down the location. More than once, the truck battery was dead or near to it, so it was pushed, towed or jumped to get it going. Sometimes we just followed the "glow in the sky" to get to the fire.

Seldom did we actually save a house, though not for lack of trying. THE BELGRADE CELLAR SAVERS became a whispered term in town, mostly in jest, but the record stood for itself. Oh yes, many large efforts were put forth and there were heroic acts. A few guys got hurt falling through roofs and ceilings. One of our few saves in that era was Don Clement's chicken house, the hero being the '39 Dodge that pumped water for hours from the dam, up over Wing's Hill lawn and behind Charlie Randall's house—the 96 horsepower flat head six seized up just as the fire got under control. Steve Judkins replaced the engine with a 120 horsepower Desoto six.

At the same time that the pumpers were being replaced, more trucks called "tankers" were needed, as running out of water was the biggest problem. Knowing that the voters might object to more new trucks, country ingenuity came into play. Guys like Bill Pulsifer, Skip Hammond, The Tukey Brothers and Bud Knowles, then later Rick Damren, built tank trucks from older trucks acquired by donation or for little money. The first tank truck was built from an old stake body truck acquired from Dow Air Force Base through Civil Defense, then fitted with an oil tank mounted on the back. North Belgrade had a tanker sporting a fish tank with quite large holes in the top, water often spilled out whenever driver Kenny Tukey slammed on the brakes. Now into the 1970's, running out of water was nearly a thing of the past. Just as the pumpers would be about empty, Duane Farnham would come blaring in with the Depot's muffler-less International tank truck, or Kenny T. with his fish tank truck. More homes and out buildings could now be saved. Dump tanks were soon set up at a fire for tankers to dump into. Mutual aid from adjoining towns became a reality and other factors like good communications to report fires, truck to truck talk, and more training for volunteers all played into the greatly improved BELGRADE FIRE DEPARTMENT. So hats off to firefighters old and new—and thanks to the guy who led the way, William P. Pulsifer, alias Willie P.P.

Jack and Annabel Gawler's camp, Holesinoggin

Nice old log camp

Chapter XII: Whatsa Camp?

Jeepers, that doesn't sound like too difficult a question. A camp is ahh, a building yes, well wait a minute, it's a place. Well, maybe it's both, or perhaps it's either, or even neither. Hmmm, guess this needs some lookin' into.

Let's see, the Student Dictionary here says 1. a place with tents or cabins for temporary shelter or 2. a place to live outdoors and sleep under the stars. O.K., that seems to make some sense, but somehow it seems to leave some stones unturned. Now, let's look and see what the Oxford English Dictionary has to say. There are several columns here, starting with the word's derivation. From the Old North French language and prior to that traced way back to the Roman era, and the Latin word "campus." Campus was then what the Romans called a field, field of tournament, field of battle, place for games—and so on. A notation was made that in 540, the youth of Rome pitched their sudden camp before their foe. Then we see encampment used and the verbatious forms: to pitch one's camp, to remain or live in a camp, to camp out. Whoa, this is getting complicated, maybe a little over our Maine heads. Let's range back into this era and look for the answer. I thought a good start would be to ask some other folks, both those that live here and some from away what "camp" means to them. You know, like what is conjured up in your mind when the word is spoken. No harm in askin'. There is nothing like starting at home. My wife, Doris, says that she's camped in tents in her youth while crossing the USA, later in a tiny towable camper, then a rustic building on a island and later in a very nice lodge. For her, the word camp is a place or a building, but more importantly, the word conjures up a common thread of positive and happy memories, which include: friends and family, outdoors, nature, good times and laughter which promote a spirit that endures a lifetime. She also points out that camps and camping are a way of life for many Mainers and also create employment in various forms.

The Bucknam family, camp owners here in Maine, had these things to say: Andy quotes his college professor as saying "a camp is a place with no running water."

Heather says "we call our place a camp as it fits in with local lingo."

Timmy says, "it's a place that is isolated and remote, not a bad thing."

Amanda says "the schedule is different at camp than at home—and there are donuts from Day's store!"

To Ralph and Jean Pope from Arrowsic, Maine, the word camp brings up images of opening their old log place in spring. "The bathtubs and sinks were often full of spiders and daddy longlegs, as well as bureau drawers with acorns and mouse poop from winter residents. There were always docks to fix, brush to cut, boats to launch and motors to start. The magic part was the future it promised; a summer of fun, fishing, and for the kids, freedom to explore and rekindle wonderful connections with friends."

Joan Witkin, summer resident from New York, lists the ingredients of her magical images of camp. She says, "of course there's the more obvious magical parts, the lake, the loons, beautiful trees and shoreline just to name a few." An added extra for Joan and her husband Bill are feelings generated from the fact they are the current owners and caretakers of a 120 year old log camp with outbuildings on a island. As the fourth owners, Joan and Bill feel a reverence for the property and for previous owners, as well as a responsibility to maintain the originality of the buildings, land and the continuity of purpose. A letter found under a table leaf from the original owner helps evidence the minimal changes to the place over a century of time. A draw full of "unidentifiable" kitchen tools and appliances also verify the desire to carry forth and maintain. Last but not least says Joan, "the bonding that has taken place here during our 30 year tenure, both with local people as well as friends and family, has created an irreplaceable common denominator."

In summing up the definition of "camp," in no short order, it seems the word means an array of many different things to many different people. We've heard definitions and ideas including: a desirable place to go that is away from home, usually away from normal work and hectic schedules. A place to kick back a bit, squander time without a schedule, a place to reconnect with old friends and meet some new. A place to rejuvenate the mind and body. A place to watch nature carry on itself and feel a part of it. A place to carry out favorite activities. All in all, it seems the word "camp" is surely not just a building, and the word "place" is by far the most commonly used. Maybe the Romans had it right. WHATSA CAMP TO YOU?

THE END

Author's Note: If you'd care to order additional copies of The Luckiest Boy 12 story series for your camp library or for gifts, call Rod or Doris Johnson for particulars at 495-3302, or e-mail us at rodorjohn@hotmail.com. Thanks again, Rod

Photo Gallery

Woodland Camp main dock looking west, c. 1930

Looking north to Mt. Phillip

Fall shore, shallow water

Fall lay-up

Ice driving on Great Pond, 1990s

Rick and Kris Johnson's camp, 1994

QUIPS AND QUOTES

Note: These sayings are a random collection, some often heard coming out of the mouths of the characters in the stories, as noted. Others are just passed around from time to time when talking with the Maine locals, and a few from summer residents. Hopefully you can find a few you have not heard! Many common ones were omitted due to foul language or content.

Lee Law—good cook, excellent fisherman, bird watcher, philosopher and friend, also a connoisseur of cheap whiskey. Best Quote: "There's 20 good drinks in every bottle—plus leakage and suckage." Lee dropped dead while walking a trap line with Gary Day around 1970, and is missed by all.

Leland J. Buzzell—excellent mechanic, father of 5 boys. Best quote when he disagreed, which was often: "Not by a god damn site."

Clifford Johnson, my Dad, carpenter, boat builder, hunter and trapper. Several good quotes were: first, when asked how he liked going to Florida: "You don't have to shovel it," second best, on a really cold day in February while shoveling camp roofs: "It's a good day for snot." Number three, when asked by a new comer what he could do to fix the newly purchased old farmhouse: "I'd start with a gallon of gas and a match" and fourthly: when kids borrowed tools, "That's got come home written all over it."

Fred Saxton—friend, good mechanic on boats or cars, Model A Ford specialist, World War II amputee. Best Quote: "I pity you bastards with two legs."

Melvin Pray—great carpenter, tile man, fisherman and

hunter. Best 3 Quotes: At 5 p.m. on a job, as he dropped his nail pouch and hammer holster: "Let's get out of here, this is cuttin' into my drinking time." Secondly: "I've been thrown off better jobs than this," and lastly, after getting turned around in the woods while hunting: "You are never lost, just someplace where you don't want to be."

Everett Johnson—respected citizen and selectman, plowed town roads for years with a big FWD, V-plow and double wings. When my cousin Skip and I told him we had the plowing contract. Best quote, "I never knew a man yet that made any money plowing snow."—He was right of course.

Byron Johnson—mechanic, hunter, and fisherman. When asked how he liked his old truck: "It wouldn't pull an old lady off a pee pot."

Carroll Gordon, alias Cabbage—good mechanic on packing plant equipment. A man of many sayings, his best two quotes are: First, when asked what he was having for lunch: "A pregnant biscuit and a hydraulic sandwich." (this was a crème roll and 2 Schlitz ales) Secondly, when consoling a teenager who was gagging while attempting to chew tobacco: "You have to be old to chew that stuff; I'm 66 and not old enough yet."

Al Meservey—could do most anything with equipment: When things weren't going well on a project or he hurt himself : "Jesus, Joseph, and Mary, four hands around."

Larry DiPetro—equipment operator, trucker. When asked how he was going to get a huge truck and equipment into a tight spot. Best Quote: "Once you get the bumper in the rest will come."

Bill Rimm—doctor and generous friend to many. Bill came up with many quotes, some of which are in the following list. A few of his favorites are: "No good deed goes unpunished," and secondly, "nervous as a long-tail cat in a room full of rocking chairs," and thirdly: "You can't teach an old dog new tricks."

Frank Hopkins—When asked in the springtime when the fish would bite: "The trout will bite when the buds on the alders are as big as a mouse's ear."

Henry Parlin—about Pepto Bismal: "That stuff's not fit to feed a hoss."

Cliff Johnson—about crooked lumber: "That board wouldn't make a good box of matchsticks." also, "No wonder this place is cold, you could throw a cat out through it most anywhere."

Note: From this point on we will present a general list that many people from here and away use upon occasion.

That's as homely as a hedge fence

It's not worth a plug nickel

Blacker than the ace of spades

Busier than a one-armed paper hanger

Smooth as a smelt

Good enough for State work

Good enough for poor folks

Colder than a well digger's butt

Scarcer than hen's teeth

Numb as a pounded thumb

Ugly as sin

It's the pot callin' the kettle black

Tougher than tripe

The road to hell was paved with good intentions

Harder than the hinges of hell

You know just enough to be dangerous

Damned if you do, damned if you don't

You can't make a silk purse out of a sow's ear

This truck rides like a buckboard

There's no rest for the weary

This smell is enough to gag a maggot

It's tougher than a bag of hammers

Straighter than a die

Looks like it was run over by a freight train

Happy as a clam

Madder than a wet hornet

That tire's only flat on one side

Couldn't hit the broad side of a barn

She's leanin' toward Sawyers

It smells so bad it would drive a hyena off a gut cart

She's some sharp

It's rainin' like a tall cow peeing on a flat rock

Lucky Boys

4 war baby cousins born in Belgrade Lakes within 2 months, 1947. Clockwise from top left, Skip Johnson, Rod Johnson, Cary Johnson, Rickey Johnson.

About the Author

Rod was born in a Waterville, Maine hospital in 1947, one of many "war babies" that came into the world in that era. Being raised by self-employed parents Clifford and Elsie Johnson on Main street in Belgrade Lakes, offered a life of considerable childhood freedom as well as adventures right from the early years.

Employment came from many different areas, but boats and motors at the family boat rental shop were a primary interest and offered jobs as a mechanic and general fixer. In later years, summer employment was at Day's Marina. Around 1980, carpentry took over as the primary employment as camps and homes were being built in the area.

Today, Rod lives with wife Doris in Rome, Maine and winters in Dunedin, Florida, near children and grandchildren. The love of boats remains and many of last 14 winters have been aboard a 41 foot Morgan sloop, and a 34 foot Mainship trawler. Also, collecting antique outboard motors and starting the Antique Outboards of Belgrade museum is high on the current list. This book is the first attempt at writing.